THE EXPRESSION OF ART

Inspired by The Holy Quran

Maira Hamid

In the name of Allah, the Beneficent, the Merciful.

The Quran is a primary source of guidance. Today it is exactly the same as it was revealed to the prophet Muhammad (PBUH) over 1400 years ago. This is because Allah had promised that He would safeguard His final revelation to mankind until the Day of Judgement. All copies of the Quran are identical, are written in the Arabic language and there can be no discrepancy between them. Also Muslims from all over the world can maneuver the Quran's Arabic. The Quran is a living miracle given by Allah to the prophet Muhammad (PBUH) and it stands as a witness to the testimony that it has withstood the test of time.

Read: In the name of your Lord Who creates,

Creates man from a clot.

Read: And your Lord is the Most Bounteous,

Who teaches by the pen,

Teaches man that he knew not,

Nay, but verily man is rebellious,

That he thinks himself independent!

To your Lord is the return.

Chapter: 96, Verses: 1-8

Contents

1 | Calligraphy…. "Allah" God

In the name of Allah, the Beneficent, the Merciful

Say: He is Allah, the One!

Allah, the Eternally Implored by all!

He begets not nor was begotten

And there is none comparable to Him.

Chapter: 112

(Size: W: 20, L: 20 inches)

(Size: W: 36, L: 72 inches)

2 | Prostration

And if you are in doubt concerning that which We reveal to
Our slave (Muhammad), then produce a Surah of the like of
it, and call your witness besides Allah if you are truthful.

Chapter: 2, Verse: 23

3 | Night and Day

In the creation of the heavens and the earth and (in) the difference of night and day are signs (of His Sovereignty) for men of understanding,

Such as remember Allah, standing, sitting and reclining, and consider the creation of the heavens and the earth, (and say): Our Lord! You created not this in vain. Glory be to you! Preserve us from the doom of Fire.

Chapter: 3, Verses: 190-191

(Size: W: 24, L: 36 inches)

4 | Final Revelation

And if you are in doubt concerning that which We reveal to Our slave (Muhammad), then produce a Surah of the like of it, and call your witness besides Allah if you are truthful.

Chapter: 2, Verse: 23

(Size: W: 36, L: 36 inches)

5 | Signs of His creation

Consider him who had an argument with Abraham about
his Lord, because Allah had given him the Kingdom; how,
when Abraham said: My Lord is He who gives life and
causes death, he answered: I give life and cause death.
Abraham said: Allah causes the sun to rise in the East,
So do you cause it to come up from the West? Thus was
the disbeliever embarrassed. And Allah guides not wrong
doing people.

Chapter: 2, Verse: 258

6 | # "Man" as Allah's best creature

Man We did create from a quintessence (of clay);

Then We placed him as (a drop of) sperm in a place
of rest, firmly fixed;

Then We made the sperm into a clot of congealed blood;
then of that cloth We made a (foetus) lump; then We made
out of that lump bones and clothed the bones with flesh;
then We developed out of it another creature. So blessed
be Allah, the best to create!

Chapter: 23, Verses: 12-14

Let there be no compulsion in religion. Truth stands out clear from error: whoever rejects false deities and believes in Allah has grasped the most trustworthy hand-hold, that never breaks. And Allah hears and knows all things.

Allah is the protector of those who have faith. From the depth of darkness He leads them into light. Of those who reject faith their patrons are the false deities, from light they will lead them forth into depth of darkness. They will be companions of the fire, to dwell therein forever.

Chapter: 2, Verses: 256-257

(Size: W: 43, L: 54 inches)

8   Butterfly of Life

Nothing is the life of the world except a pastime and a sport. Better far is the abode of the Hereafter for those who keep their duty (to Allah). Have you then no sense?

Chapter: 6, Verse: 32

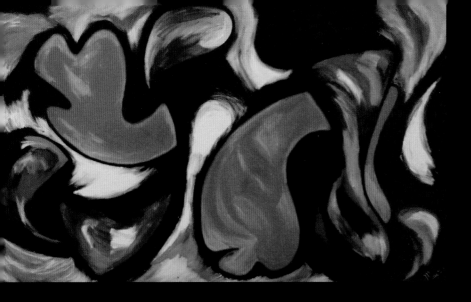

For that cause We decreed for the children of Israel that whoever kills a human being for other than killing or corruption in the earth, it shall be as if he had killed all mankind, and whoever saves the life of one, it shall be as if he had saved the life of all mankind. Our messengers came to them of old with clear proofs (of Allah's Sovereignty), but afterwards many of them became prodigals in the earth.

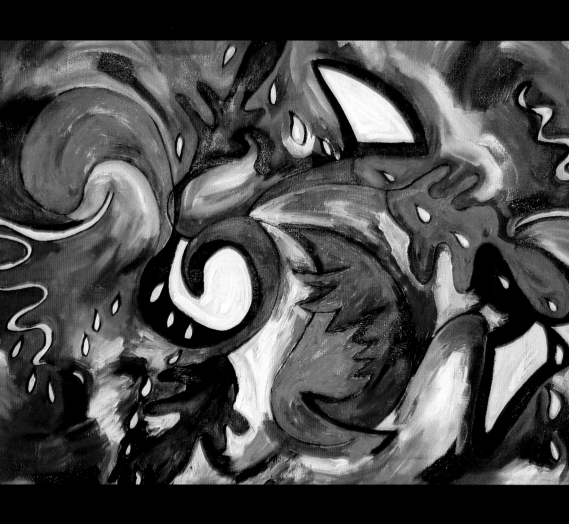

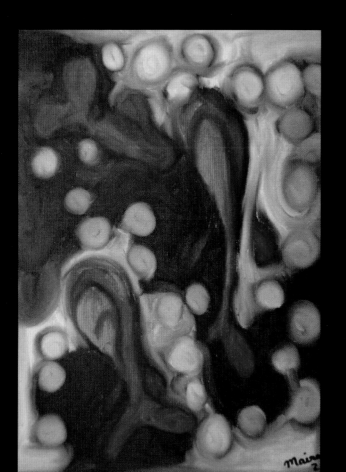

And let not those who disbelieve imagine that the rein We (God) give them is good for their souls. We only give them rein that they may grow in sinfulness. And theirs will be a shameful doom.

It is not (the purpose) of Allah to leave you in your present state till He shall separate the wicked from the good. And it is not (the purpose of) Allah to let you know the Unseen. But Allah chooses of His messengers whom He will (to receive knowledge of it). So believe in Allah and His messengers. If you believe and ward off (evil), yours will be a vast reward.

Chapter: 3, Verses: 178-179

11 | Extreme Failure

A similitude of those who disbelieve in their Lord:
Their works are as ashes which the wind blows hard
upon a stormy day. They have no control of anything
that they have earned. That is the extreme failure.

Have you not seen that Allah (God) has created the
heavens and the earth with truth? If He will, He can
remove you and bring (in) some new creation.

Chapter: 14, Verses: 18-19

(Size: W: 24, L: 36 inches)

(Size: W: 29, L: 29 inches)

12 Sea

Say: Though the sea became ink for the Words of my Lord, verily the sea would be used up before the words of my Lord were exhausted, even though We brought the like of it to help.

Say: I am only a mortal like you. My Lord inspires in me that your God is only One God. And whoever hopes for the meeting with his Lord, let him do righteous work, and make none sharer of the worship due to his Lord.

Chapter: 18, Verses: 109-110

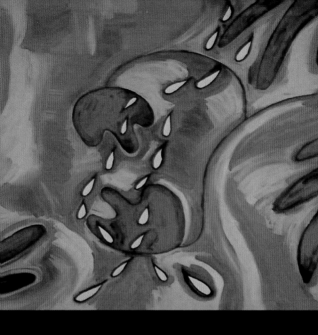

Who have believed and whose hearts have

rest in the remembrance of Allah. Verily in the

remembrance of Allah do hearts find rest!

(Size: W: 25.5, L: 35 inches)

14 | Evil and Good

Say: the evil and the good are not alike even though the plenitude of evil attracts you. So be mindful of your duty to Allah (God), O men of understanding, that you may succeed.

Chapter: 5, Verse: 100

(Size: W: 24, L: 36 inches)

15 | Final Destination

Say O People of the Scripture! You have nothing (of guidance) till you observe the Torah and the Gospel and that which was revealed to you from your Lord. That which is revealed to you (Muhammad) from your is Lord is certain to increase the rebellion and disbelief of many of them. But grieve not for the disbelieving people.

Those who believe, and those who are Jews, and Sabaeans, and Christians-whoever believes in Allah and the Last Day and does right-no fear shall come upon them neither shall they grieve..

Chapter: 5, Verses: 68-69

(Size: W:29, L: 29 inches)

(Size: W: 43, L: 54 inches)

16 | Equality

Men who surrender to Allah, and women who surrender,

and men who believe and women who believe, and men

who obey and women who obey, and men who speak

the truth and women who speak the truth, and men who

persevere (in righteousness) and women who persevere,

and men who are humble and women who are humble, and

men who give alms and women who give alms, and men

who fast and women who fast, and men who guard (their

modesty), and women who guard (their modesty), and men

who remember Allah much and women who remember.

Allah has prepared for them forgiveness and a vast reward.

Chapter: 33, Verse: 35

17 | Hides

Now they fold up their hearts that they may hide (their thoughts) from Him (God). At the very moment when they cover themselves with their clothing, Allah knows that which they keep hidden and that which they proclaim. He is Aware of what is in the hearts (of men).

Chapter: 11, Verse: 5

(Size: W: 24, L: 36 inches)

18 | Favours

Which is it, of the favours of your

Lord, that you deny

Chapter: 55, Verse: 13

(Size, W: 36, L: 26 inches)

19 | Honey

And your Lord inspired the bee, saying: Choose habitations
in the hills and in the trees and in that which they thatch;

Then eat of all fruits, and follow the ways of your Lord,
made smooth (for you). There comes out from their bellies
a drink of diverse hues, in which is healing for mankind. In
this is indeed a sign for people who reflect.

Chapter: 16, Verses: 68-69

(Size: W: 43; L: 54 inches)

(Size: W: 43, L: 54 inches)

20   Marriage

And if you fear that you will not deal fairly with the
orphans, marry of the women, who seem good to
you, two or three or four; and if you fear that you
cannot do justice (to so many) then one (only) or
(the captives) that your right hands posses. Thus it
is more likely that you will not do injustice.

And give to the women (whom you marry) free
gift of their marriage portions; but if they of their
own accord remit to you a part of it, then you are
welcome to absorb it (in your wealth)

Chapter: 4, Verses: 3-4

And Satan says, when the matter has been
decided: Allah promised you a promise of truth;
and I promised you, then failed you.
And I had no power over you
except that I called to you and you obeyed me.
So blame me not, but blame yourselves.
I cannot help you, nor can you help me,
I disbelieved in that which you before
ascribed to me.
For wrongdoers is a painful doom.

Chapter: 14, Verse: 22   °

(Size: W: 35, L: 25 inches)

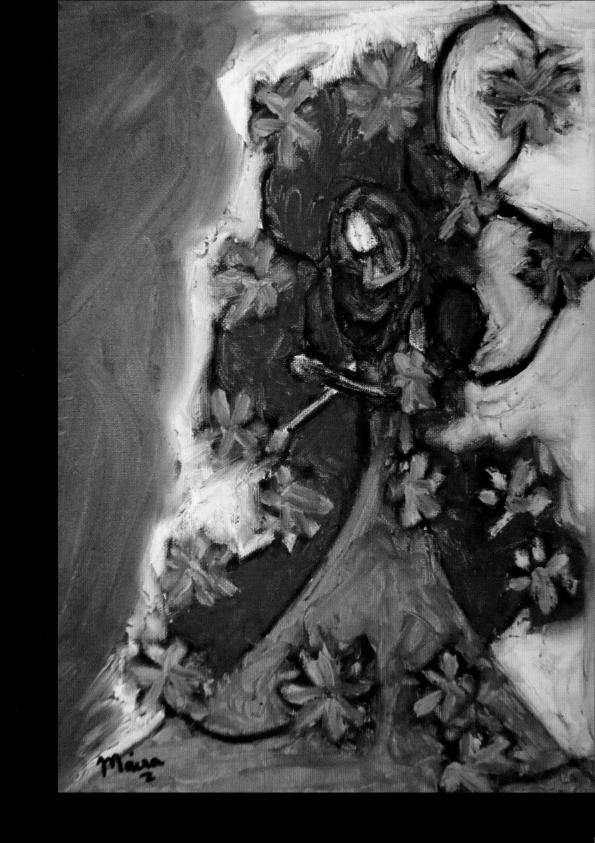

22 | World's Heaven

Who has created seven heavens in harmony.
You (Muhammad) can see no fault in the
Beneficent One's Creation; then look again:
can you see any rifts?

Then look again and yet again, your sight
will return to you weakened and made dim.

And verily We have beautified the world's
heaven with lamps, and We have made
them missiles for the devils, and for them
We have prepared the doom of flame.

And for those who disbelieve in their Lord
there is the doom of Hell, an unhappy
journey's end!

Chapter: 67, Verses: 3-6

(Size: W:24, L: 36 inches)

23 | Relations

And He it is Who has created man from water, and has appointed for him relatives by blood and relatives by marriage; for your Lord is ever Powerful.

Yet they worship instead of Allah that which can neither benefit them nor hurt them. The disbeliever was ever a partisan against his Lord.

And We have sent you (O Muhammad) only as a bearer of good tidings and a warner.

Chapter: 25, Verses: 54-56

(Size: W: 36, L: 60 inches)

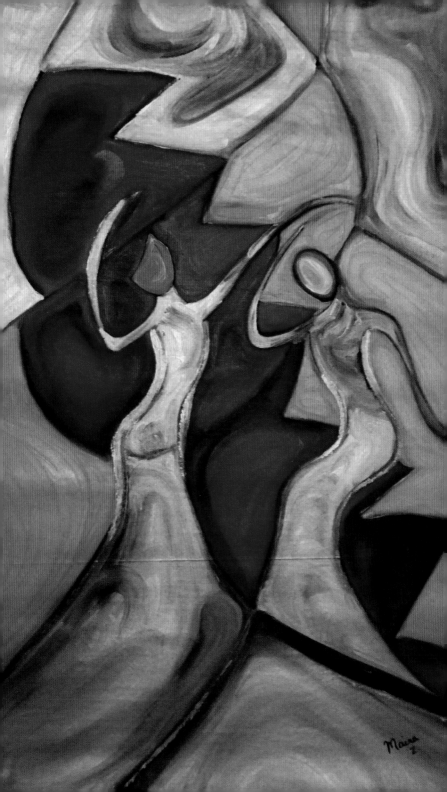

Fight in the way of Allah against those who
fight against you, but transgress not the limits.
Truly, Allah likes not the transgressors.

Chapter: 2, Verse: 190

(Size: W: 36, L: 36 inches)

25 | Partners

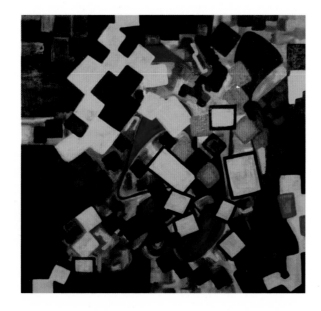

And when harm touches men they call to their Lord, turning to Him in repentance; then, when they have tasted of His mercy, some of them attribute partners to their Lord.

So as to disbelieve in that which We have given them. (to such it is said): Enjoy yourselves a while, but you will come to know.

Or have We revealed to them any authority which speaks of that which they associate with Him?

And when We cause mankind to taste of mercy they rejoice in it; but if an evil thing befalls them as the consequence of their own deeds, they are in despair!

Do they not see that Allah enlarges the provision for whom He wills, and tightens (it for whom He wills). In this indeed are signs for people who believe.

Chapter: 30, Verses: 33-37

(Size: W: 36, L: 36 inches)

26 | Helpless Souls

A soul will know what it has sent before
(it) and what left behind:

O man! What has made you careless
concerning your Lord, the Bountiful,

Who created you, then fashioned you,
then proportioned you?

Into whatever form He will, He casts you.

Nay, but you deny the Judgement.

Chapter: 82, Verses: 5-9

(Size: W: 36, L: 36 inches)

27   Life and Death

Blessed is He in whose hand is the
Sovereignty, and He is Able to do all things.

Who has created life and death that He may
try you which of you is best in conduct; and
He is the Mighty, the Forgiving.

Chapter: 67, Verses: 1-2

(Size: W: 43, L: 54 inches)

28 | Harm Touches

(O mankind) your Lord is He who drives for you the ship upon the sea that you may seek of His bounty. He was ever Merciful towards you.

And when harm touches you upon the sea, all to whom you call (for help) fail except Him (alone), but when He brings you safe to land, you turn away, for man was ever thankless

He has created the heavens without supports that you can
see, and has cast into the earth firm hills, so that it does
not quake with you; and He has dispersed in it all kinds
of beasts. And We send down water from the sky and We
cause (plants) of every goodly kind to grow in it.

This is the creation of Allah. Now show me that which
those (you worship) besides Him have created. Nay, but
the wrongdoers are in manifest error!

30 | Beauty of Woman

And tell the believing women to lower their
gaze and be modest, and to display of their
adornment only that which is apparent, and
to draw their veils over their chests, and not to
reveal their adornment except to their
own husbands or fathers or...

Chapter: 24, Verse: 31

And those who, when they do an evil thing or wrong themselves, remember Allah and implore forgiveness for their sins – who forgives sins except Allah only? And will not knowingly repeat (the wrong) they did.

The reward of such will be forgiveness from their Lord, and Gardens underneath which rivers flow, in which they will remain forever- a bountiful reward for workers!

(Size: W: 43, L: 54 inches)

32 | The Declining Day

By the declining day,

Man is in a state of loss,

Except those who believe and do good works, and exhort
one another to truth and exhort one another to endurance.

Chapter: 103, Verses: 1-3

33   Fear of Allah

If We had caused this Quran to descend upon a
mountain, you (O Muhammad) verily would have seen it
humbled, spilt apart by the fear of Allah. Such similitudes
We coin for mankind that perhaps they may reflect.

He is Allah, other than Whom there is no God, the
Knower of the Invisible and the Visible. He is the
Beneficent, Merciful.

Chapter: 59, Verses: 21-22

(Size: W: 35.5, L: 25 inches)

34 | Revelations

Allah! There is no God except Him, the Alive, the Eternal.

He has revealed to you (Muhammad) the scripture with truth, confirming that which was (revealed) before it, even as He revealed the Torah and the Gospel.

Chapter: 3, Verses: 2-3

O you who have believed, be persistently standing firm in justice, witnesses for Allah, even if it be against yourselves or parents and relatives. Whether one is rich or poor, Allah is more worthy of both. So follow not (personal) inclination, lest you not be just. And if you distort (your testimony) or refuse (to give it), then indeed Allah is ever, with what you do, Acquainted.

Chapter: 4, Verse: 135

And if any one of idolaters seeks your protection (O Muhammad), then protect him so that he may hear the Word of Allah, and afterwards convey him to his place of safety. That is because they are a people who know not.

Chapter: 9, Verse: 6

37 | Sacred Life

Say: Come, I will recite to you that which your Lord has
made a sacred duty for you: That you ascribe no thing
as Partner to Him and that you do good to parents, and
that you slay not your children because of destitution-
We provide for you and for them- and that you draw
not near to lewd things whether open or concealed.
And that you slay not the life which Allah has made
sacred, except in the course of justice. This He has
commanded you, in order that you may discern.

Chapter: 6, Verse: 151

(Size: W: 24, L: 24 inches)

38 Unity

And hold fast, all of you together, to the rope of Allah, and do not separate. And remember Allah's favour to you: how you were enemies and He made friendship between your hearts so that you became as brothers by His grace; and (how) you were upon the brink of an abyss of fire, and He did save you from it. Thus Allah makes clear His revelations to you, that perhaps you may be guided.

Chapter: 3, Verse: 103

39 | Only a Messenger

And when Our clear revelations are recited to them,
they who look not for the meeting with Us say:
Bring a Lecture other than this, or change it. Say
(O Muhammad): It is not for me to change it of my
accord. I only follow that which is inspired in me. If I
disobey my Lord, I fear the retribution of an awful Day.

Say: If Allah had so willed I should not have recited
it to you nor would He have made it known to you.
I dwelt among you a whole lifetime before it (came
to me). Have you then no sense?

Chapter: 10, Verses: 15-16

(Size: W: 24, L: 20 inches)

40 | Ponder

And of them are some who listen to you. But can you make the deaf to hear even though they apprehend not?

And of them is he who looks towards you. But can you guide the blind even though they see not?

Allah does not wrong mankind in anything; but mankind wrong themselves.

Chapter: 10, Verses: 42-44

(Size: W: 24, L: 36 inches)

41 | A new Life

And they say: When we are bones and fragments, shall we be raised up as a new creation?

Say: Be you stones or iron.

Or some created thing that is yet greater in your thoughts! Then they will say: Who shall bring us back (to life). Say He Who created you at the first. Then they will shake their heads at you, and say: When will it be? Say: It will perhaps be soon.

A day when He will call you and you will answer with His praise, and you will think that you have stayed but a little while.

Chapter: 17, Verses: 49-52

(Size: W: 24, L: 36 inches)

(Size: W: 25.5, L: 35 inches)

(Remember) when Abraham said to his father Azar:
Do you take idols for gods? I see you and your people
in error manifest.

Thus did We show Abraham the Kingdom of the
heavens and the earth that he might be of those
possessing certainly.

When the night grew dark upon him he saw a star.
He said: This is my Lord. But when it set, he said: I
love not things that set.

And when he saw the moon rising, he exclaimed: This
is my Lord. But when it set, he said: Unless my Lord
guides me, I surely shall become one of the people
who are astray.

And when he saw sun rising, he exclaimed: This is
my Lord! This is greater! And when it set he
exclaimed: O my people! I am free from all that you
associate (with Him).

I have turned my face towards Him Who created the
heavens and the earth, as one by nature upright,
and I am not of the idolaters.

His people argued with him. He said: Dispute you
with me concerning Allah when He has guided me?
I fear not at all that which you set up besides Him
unless my Lord wills in any way. My Lord includes
all things in His knowledge. Will you not then
remember?

How should I fear that which you set up besides Him,
when you fear not to set up besides Allah that for
which He has revealed to you no authority? Which
of the two factions has more right to safety?
(Answer me that) if you have knowledge.

Those who believe and obscure not their belief
by wrongdoing, theirs is safety; and they are
rightly guided.

That is Our argument. We gave it to Abraham against
his people. We raise to degrees of wisdom whom We
will. Your Lord is Wise, Aware.

Chapter: 6, Verses: 74-83

43 | Believing Man

Tell the believing men to lower their gaze
and be modest. That is purer for them.
Allah is aware of what they do.

Chapter: 24, Verse: 30

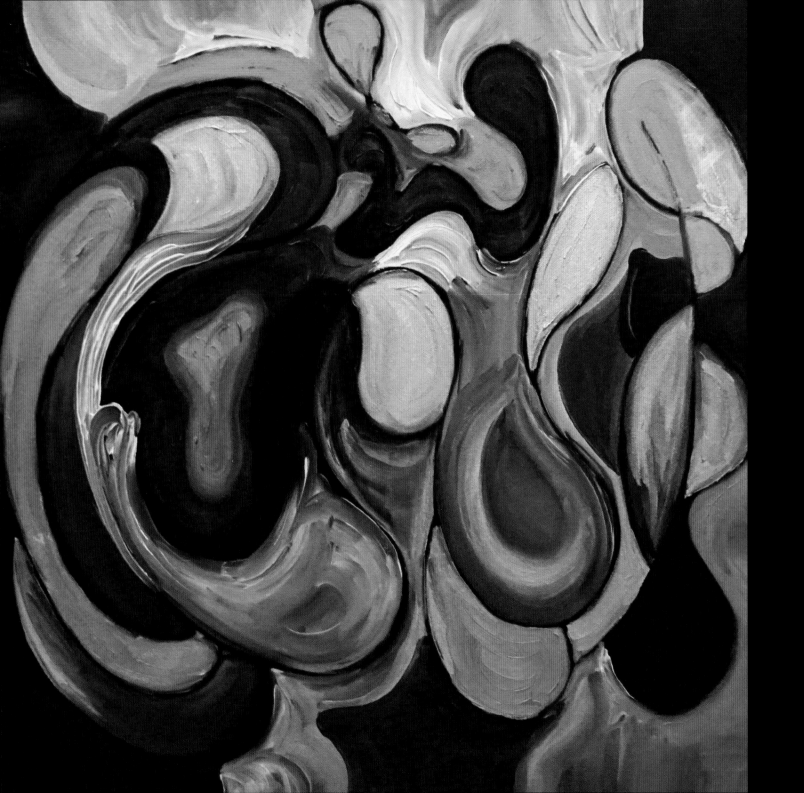

44 | Returned to your Lord

Have not those who disbelieve know that the
heavens and the earth were of one piece, then We
parted them, and We made every living thing of
water? Will they not then believe?

And We have placed in the earth firm hills lest it
quake with them, and We have placed in it ravines
as roads that perhaps they may find their way.

And We have made the sky a roof withheld (from
them). Yet they turn away from its signs.

And He it is Who created the night and the day, and
the sun and the moon. They float, each in an orbit.

We appointed immortality for no mortal before
you. What! If you die can they be immortal.

Every soul must taste death, and We try you
with evil and with good, for ordeal. And to Us
you will returned.

Chapter: 21, Verses: 30-35

45 | Signs

We shall show them Our signs on the horizons and
within themselves until it will be manifest to them
that it is the Truth. Does your Lord not suffice,
since He is Witness over all things?

How! Are they still in doubt about the meeting
with their Lord? Is not He surrounding all things?

Chapter: 41, Verses: 53-54

(Size: W: 24, L: 24 inches)

(Size: W: 24, L: 24 inches)

46 | The purpose of Life

I created the jinn and humankind only
that they might worship Me.

I seek no livelihood from them, nor do I
ask that they should feed Me.

Allah! He it is that gives livelihood, the
Lord of unbreakable might.

Chapter: 51, Verses: 56-58

47 | Why does not Allah speak to us

And those who have no knowledge say: Why does
not Allah speak to us, or some sign come to us? Even
thus, as they now speak, spoke those (who were)
before them. Their hearts are all alike. We have made
clear the revelations for people who are sure.

Chapter: 2, Verse: 118

(Size: W: 36, L: 36 inches)

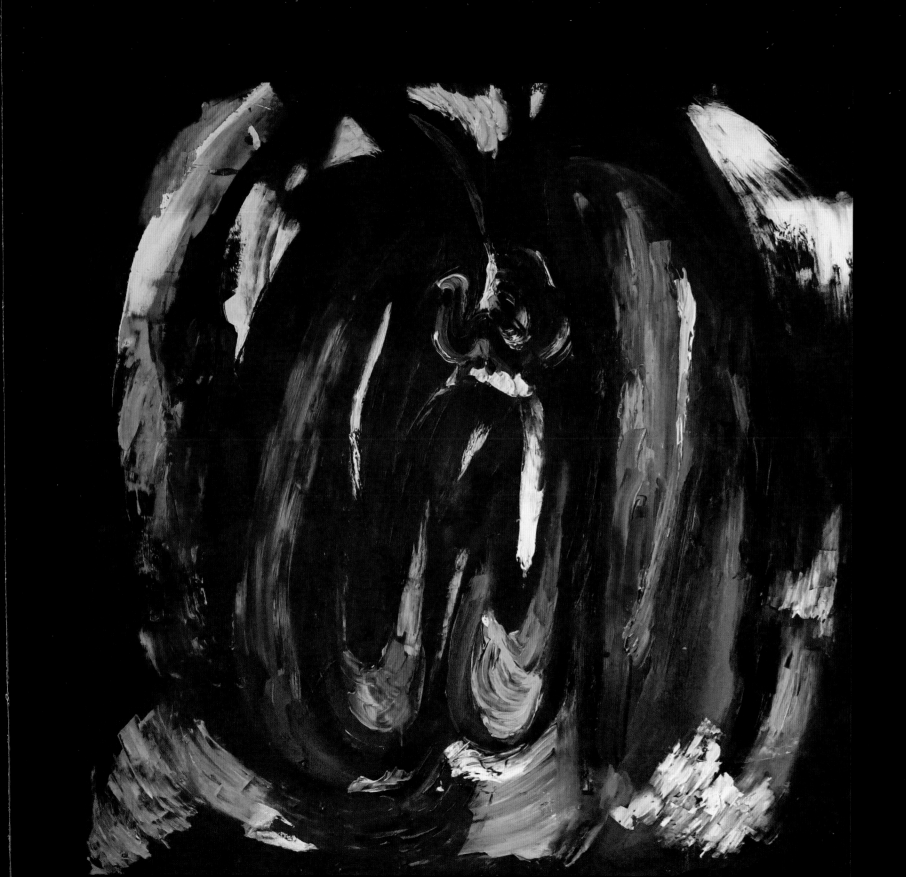

48 | Blind Hearts

Have they not travelled in the
land, and have they hearts with
which to feel and ears with which
to hear? For indeed it is not
the eyes that grow blind, but it is the
hearts, which are within the
bosoms, that grow blind.

Chapter: 22, Verse: 46

49   Life

How do you disbelieve in Allah when you were dead
and He gave life to you? Then He will give you death,
then life again, and then to Him you will return.

Chapter: 2, Verses: 28

(Size: W: 10, L: 14 inches)

50   Taste of Death

Every soul will taste death.

And you will be paid on the day of

Resurrection only that which you have fairly

earned. Whoever is removed from the Fire and is

made to enter Paradise, he is indeed is triumphant.

The life of this world is only comfort of illusion."

Chapter: 3, Verse: 185

As for those who defame virtuous, believing women (who are) unaware, cursed are they in the world and the Hereafter. Theirs will be an awful doom.

On the day when their tongues and their hands and their feet testify against them as to what they used to do.

On that day Allah will pay them their just due, and they will know that Allah, He is the Manifest Truth.

Vile women are for vile men, and vile men for vile women. Good women are for good men, and good men for good women; such are innocent of that which people say: For them is pardon and a bountiful provision.

Chapter: 24, Verses: 23-26

52 | Reflect

Assuredly, the creation of the heavens and the earth
is greater than the creation of mankind; but most of
mankind know not.

And the blind man and the seer are not equal, neither
are those who believe and do good works (equal
with) the evil-doer. Little do you reflect!

Chapter: 40, Verses: 57-58

53 | Adam's Ale

Have you observed the water which you drink?

Is it you who shed it from the rain cloud,
or are We the shedder?

If We willed, We verily could make it bitter.
Why then, do you not give thanks?

Chapter: 56, Verses: 68-70

(Size: W: 10, L: 14 inches)

(Size: W: 14, L: 10 inches)

And when your Lord said to the angels: I am about to place a viceroy in the earth, they said: Will you place in it one who will do harm in it and will shed blood, while we, we hymn Your praise and sanctify You? He said: surely I know that which you know not.

And He taught Adam all the names, then showed them to the angels, saying: Inform Me of the names, if you are truthful.

They said: Be glorified! We have no knowledge except that which You have taught us. You, only You, are the Knower, the Wise.

He said: O Adam! Inform them of their names, and when he had informed them of their names, He said: Did I not tell you that I know the secret of the heavens and the earth? And I know that which you disclose and which you hide.

And when We said to the angels: Prostrate yourselves before Adam, they fell prostrate, all except Iblis (satan). He demurred through pride, and so became a disbeliever.

We said: O Adam! Dwell you and your wife in the Gardens, and eat you freely (of the fruits) of it where you will; but come not near this tree lest you become wrongdoers.

But satan caused them to deflect from it and expelled them from the (happy) state in which they were; and We said: Fall down, one of you a foe to the other! There shall be for you on earth a habitation and provision for a time.

Then Adam received from his Lord words (of revelation), and He relented towards him. He is the Relenting, the Merciful.

We said: Go down, all of you, from here; so when there comes to you from Me a guidance, no fear shall come upon them, neither shall they grieve.

But they who disbelieve, and deny Our revelations, such are rightful peoples of the Fire. They will remain in it.

When they listen to that which has been revealed
to the messengers, you see their eyes overflow with
tears because of their recognition of the Truth.
They say: Our Lord, we believe. Inscribe us
as among the witness.

How should we not believe in Allah and that which
has come to us of the Truth. And (how should we
not) hope that our Lord will bring us in along with
righteous people?

Allah has rewarded them on account of their
saying- Gardens underneath which rivers flow, in
which they will remain forever. That is the reward
of the good."

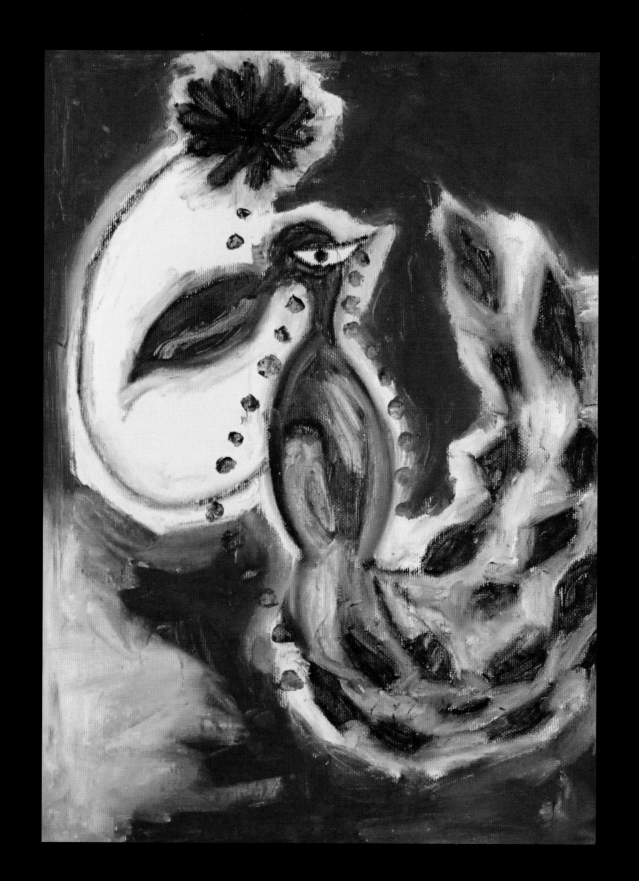

Praise be to Allah, Lord of the Worlds.

Maira Hamid © The Expression of Art
First published 2016 by Maira Hamid
ISBN: 978-0-9934897-0-9

Maira's Art
Original Oil Paintings

Maira's Gallery London
facebook.com/mairasgallerylondon
facebook.com/mairasartlondon

Designed by Bobby&Co
Printed in China